How to Get a Job in Web Development

RealToughCandy

"Never Trust the YouTube Comments."

-Ancient Chinese Proverb

Table of Contents

Preface

When I started my web development journey, I was a lost hiker in the digital woods. I knew I wanted to build web apps, but didn't know what those people called themselves. Were they website builders? Programmers? The term "software engineer" floated around a lot online – was that my aspiration?

Since I didn't know exactly what I was looking for, I spent a lot of time reading and watching materials that were nothing but discouraging: mock Google coding interviews with whiteboards and markers. Lots of articles and videos that name-dropped things like binary trees, Big O notation, and time complexity. Forum post upon forum post that gave away actual coding interview questions from the biggest tech companies in the world like Facebook, Google, and Microsoft.

None of it made sense to me, even though I had been studying and practicing HTML, CSS, and JavaScript. During that painful stretch, I ended up learning what we actually call ourselves – *web developers*. That helped narrow my search when it came to learning resources, but YouTube was still suggesting some heavy engineering videos.

Making things worse, some web developers I had discovered on YouTube were talking about a popular book for coding interviews. I checked it out and once again my stomach sank. "I'm never going to make it in this field," I said to myself. "I've been studying and practicing and building projects for months and I still have no idea what these people are talking about." What they didn't tell me was that the book is geared towards senior software engineers trying to get a job with Amazon and Google.

I wanted to quit my coding journey. In fact, I did quit. The difference was, I didn't *stay* quit. Something told me to keep pushing forward, keep building projects to put in my portfolio and on GitHub, keep reaching out and trying to find clients who needed websites. I kept pushing until I got a job as a fullstack web developer at a data company.

As it turns out, the web isn't very generous to our career field. Beginners are especially marginalized. There aren't any quality one-stop resources for discovering the answer to one of the most important questions – if not *the* most important question – web developers have: "How do I get a job in this field?"

I wanted to change the junior web developer tech landscape with this book. My goal is for every junior developer who reads it to find a job. And if you take the recommended actions in this book, you **can** do it.

How to Get a Job in Web Development is designed for junior web developers. Whether you're coming from a coding bootcamp, are completely self-taught, or graduated from college with a tech-related degree, this book is for you.

No awkward whiteboard interviews.

No hour-long explanation of Big O notation.

Just practical, actionable steps that will put you far ahead of the pack when it comes to getting a job in web development.

Two important assumptions

This book assumes you will pursue a full-time web development job. Freelancing, contracting, and gigs aren't discussed.

This book assumes you have, or plan on having, the basic technical knowledge necessary for an entry-level job in web development:

For those on the frontend development track, your technical knowledge includes HTML5, CSS3, and client-side JavaScript. It also includes a frontend framework such as React, Angular, or Vue.

For those on the backend development track, your technical knowledge includes server-side technologies that fuel the functionality of applications. A few examples of this track include the LAMP (Linux, Apache, MySQL, PHP) stack; Node.js; Ruby/RoR; and Python/Django.

For those on the fullstack development track, this includes frontend and backend technologies. Two examples of a fullstack development track include the MERN stack (MongoDB, Express, React, Node) and the MEAN stack (MongoDB, Express, Angular, Node).

I'm *very* new to development...Should I even be reading this?

Yes! Even if you haven't studied the basics of HTML yet, early preparation is going to make the job application process so much smoother. Eventually, when you *do* see a job opening you're ready to apply to, you'll know exactly what to do. You won't be wasting hours or even days trying to think of a clever way to present your portfolio, or how to craft your resume and cover letter so that employers want to meet you. You can simply reference this manual whenever you need guidance.

What about WordPress jobs?

WordPress is a special consideration. Powering over 30% of the web, WordPress developers are always in demand. As WordPress is often powered by the LAMP stack, this book will also help you on your journey to secure a job as a WordPress developer. While WordPress positions can pay less than other junior web development jobs, they can be an excellent gateway to your next job that pays more and entails more responsibilities as a developer. Remember, this is a fast industry and it's not uncommon to frequently switch companies in exchange for an increased salary and better opportunities.

With that, welcome to *How to Get a Job in Web Development*.

Introduction

Does this situation sound familiar?

You're browsing the web developer job openings on Indeed.com. A few catch your eye; you click to see more about the position. The company is looking for a junior frontend web developer specializing in React. Everything is looking good, until you read further and see that they want somebody with a college degree, at least three years of experience, and they have a huge list of additional skills considered "nice-to-have."

Or how about this one?

You're curious about web development jobs and check out YouTube. You discover a few popular web development videos with titles like "Top ten highest-paying programming languages in 2018," "Learn Python in 15 minutes," and "Google Developer Whiteboard Interview." Every click of a video leads you into a deeper and darker rabbit hole, and all the conflicting and incomplete information makes you question whether or not this career field is even meant for you.

Odds are, if you're a web developer curious about jobs, you've ran into one of these scenarios. It's frustrating, it's discouraging, and it's overwhelming. Sometimes it makes you want to quit.

The truth is, the Internet is filled with a lot of inaccuracies when it comes to realistic job information for web developers. This is for many reasons (clickbait, uninformed content creators, educators with poor communication skills) - but no matter what the reason, it's damaging to developers' enthusiasm for programming.

In addition, there are a few popular resources recommended to web developers that focus on advanced algorithms or senior software engineer-style challenges. Most jobs for junior web developers aren't like that. **At all.**

In the bubble of web-based research, it's easy to get the impression that web developer jobs are only for geniuses, that they only pay well in New York City or Silicon Valley, and/or consist of coders rapidly pumping out thousands of lines of code in a day while surviving on nothing but espresso, Instagram photo filters, and bespoke chewing gum. All of these situations are false. There's room for *you* in this field – and plenty of it.

Jobs are Waiting for You

Aside from the traditional job hunting process of searching online job boards, there are other ways to find jobs in web development: in-person networking, recruiters on LinkedIn, even Twitter-searching for dev job opportunities. This book shows you what you need no matter how you find an opportunity. Now let's go get that web developer job!

Chapter 1

Introduction to the Holy Clover

When applying for web developer jobs, there are four major components you need to include: your resume, cover letter, Github page, and portfolio.

While cover letters and Github account links are often optional (and even portfolio links are many times optional), these four elements are going to create the cohesive idea that you are coding web-based projects that matter. More specifically, when executed correctly, they are going to give employers the impression that you can either save the company money; make the company money; or even more enticing, save **and** make the company money.

In this section (Chapters 1-5), we're exploring how to **architect, develop, and deploy your resume, cover letter, Github page, and portfolio**. Even better, we will craft them in a way so that key personnel will be compelled to learn more about you. These components are called the holy clover because the four of them combined create a special energy when executed correctly. When *not* executed correctly, the holy clover quickly disintegrates into a shapeless and weak entity that doesn't instill confidence in your potential employer. Take this scenario as an example.

Red's been applying to web developer jobs for months. She's hanging out a coffee shop, coding on her laptop when a professional-looking stranger approaches her. He quickly glances at Red's open code editor, taking note of her JavaScript efforts and says: "My company is hiring a web developer. Looks like you might have the skills to help us. Meet me here tomorrow, same time. We'll talk."

Thinking maybe she'd slipped into a caffeine-induced fantasy, Red shakes her head, but agrees to meet.

The next day, Red and the mystery man find a table and settle in. "So, tell me about yourself," he says, unblinking.

"Well, erm, well… I started off doing this web development thing because I was sick of my old career," Red admits, still a little unsure of herself despite saying the same thing in interviews many times before.

"There wasn't any room for growth; I was bored; my co-workers didn't understand technology or even care about it. But I love the web," she continues, "so I started studying HTML, CSS, and JavaScript...I made a few websites that are kind of cool. I found this online training course that helped me and sometimes I ask questions there and answer peoples' questions on a forum."

She's looking for some sort of visual clue that the man is still interested, but his eyes are infinite pools of unbiased binary truth. He hasn't walked off yet, so Red continues:

"I finished one of the courses and even took on a freelance project for a family member. She has a dog walking business. Then I did two websites for my own personal projects; they're OK. But this project right here," she says, opening up her laptop and pointing to her code editor, "This is the real deal. My aunt started getting some traffic and needed a rework of the frontend. So I'm rewriting it in React. I love it."

One eyebrow raised, the recruiter asks if there's anything else she'd like to share or ask.

"Oh yeah, I have a little YouTube channel where I'm sharing my journey. It's mostly just me talking about my coding adventures but I also do some React how-to videos."

With a single nod, the man walks out of the door, just as quickly and quietly as he appeared to her.

Red never hears from him again.

While this scenario sounds mildly ridiculous, it is exactly what happens when most junior web developers hit the "submit" button on an application.

Autopsy Time: Where Your Competition Fumbles

The earliest mistake candidates make in the application process is not reviewing the job or researching the company before applying. Notice how the developer in the above scenario didn't ask any questions before sharing her life as a developer. What if the company was notorious for disrespecting its employees, or was responsible for creating websites with content you didn't believe in? Would you still want to invest your time applying to the job?

Further, just like in the scenario, developers' holy clovers are often unstructured. They forget to extract the value created from their efforts; metrics take a backseat to subjective values. All these early mistakes add up, causing the developer to blend in with the long line of candidates applying for that same job.

Despite these oversights, it's not the lack of experience holding this candidate back from a junior web development position; Red doesn't need to search for more freelance clients or build any more portfolio-worthy projects. Instead, she needs to review her previous efforts and extract the important parts, phrasing them in a way that is attractive to employers.

We'll begin this restructuring process by starting with your resume.

Chapter 2

Resume Revamp

Your job is to create a resume that makes an *impact*. You'll want to focus on your technical abilities and relevant non-technical abilities while continuously encouraging the reader to learn more about you. In addition, you'll want to show how you made your clients money, saved your clients money, or if you don't have clients, how you improved a process while solving a problem. You want to show that you're capable and motivated.

Here's an example of a resume that employers love to see:

Michelle Belle
MERN Developer

Ph: 555-555-5555

michelle@michellebelle.com
www.michellebelle.com
@memchelle

Profile

Hello Company R! I know you're busy, so **here's what you need to know about me in one sentence:**

Your company stands out to me; since 2016 I've been designing and developing MERN web apps; I'm active in the open source community; my proudest moment was reaching my 700th fork for a tool I built for Express, helping save developers thousands of hours of dev time.

Relevant Experience

Freelance MERN developer - 2016 to present
Fullstack development serving a global client base.
-Conversion of a high-traffic ecommence site from PHP backend to Node ecosystem, saving $8,000 in annual maintenance fees. Conversion decreased page load time by 30%.
-Creator of MERNFlush, allowing reuse of services such as batching operations (not currently possible using Express). Forked over 700 times on GitHub.

Falls River Content Creators - 2016-present
Freelance site maintenance and digital design.
-Designed and prototyped blog section for YeOldeWharf.com; mobile-first approach caters to audience consisting of 62% mobile users.
-Conversion to HTML5 canvas from Flash for interactive posts increased user interaction by 60% in a three-month period.
-Tech employed: HTML5, CSS3, jQuery, JavaScript, Git

United States Navy- 2012-2016
Award-winning combat correspondent.
-Produced over 85 videos for global audience seen by over 1 million people (military and civilian), helping influence popular opinion on global issues.
-Produced media products with minimal supervision, saving supervisor over 10 hours a week in direct supervision duties.

Education:

Udacity — Udacity Nanodegree, Fullstack Web Development (2017)
Pretty Good College — Bachelor's, Public Health (2014)

Soft Skills:

Quick to adapt to changing technical priorities with minimal supervision.

References:

References and select client list available upon request.

Github:
Portfolio:

www.github.com/michellebelle
www.michellebelle.com

Breaking it Down

Let's break down each component.

Design: "Curb appeal" is a real estate term meaning the attractiveness of a home viewed from the street. Michelle gave her resume its own curb appeal by giving the blocks of text more room to breathe. She emphasized sections using contrast and bold lettering.

Profile: This section is a summary of who she is professionally. Her job here is easing the reader into the bulk of the document by briefly stating her experience and skills.

Experience: Michelle described her projects and duties, explained her actions, and shared the result. She included a job outside of web development, where she developed highly-valuable soft skills.

Some notes for perfecting your own experience section:

- This can be a tough one to organize for developers, especially if you don't have a lot of experience. No experience is too insignificant to include, so if your only experience is coding personal projects, include those.

- Always try to include metrics. In other words, what impact have you made? Where have you improved efficiency, saved money, or made money? For example, maybe traffic to a website you re-built went up 26% in six months after you took steps to improve page speed and user experience. Include the tools and techniques used in these improvements. Google Analytics is an excellent tool to measure many metrics.

- If you still find your experience section a little thin after listing your personal projects, freelance projects, and former tech-related employers where you had experiences with development, you can also list positions that entailed some aspect of the web development environment, process, or culture. For example, let's say you were an emergency dispatcher. Dispatching requires discipline, teamwork, and impeccable communication skills, all of which are highly-valued soft skills in web development. Do a review of your current and past positions and see if those required skill sets match up with required skills in development. Here are some skills you may have used at previous jobs:

-Communication
-Flexibility

16

-Management
-Teamwork
-Timeliness
-Process-oriented Thinking
-Teaching and/or Mentoring
-Troubleshooting
-Visual Thinking
-Conflict Resolution
-Adaptability

Education: Michelle listed a "nanodegree" related to her developer education in addition to her highest level of formal education achieved. Just like in the Experience section, no achievement is too small. Include any formal recognition of your training, whether it's a Udacity nanodegree, a certificate of completion from Treehouse or freeCodeCamp, a local coding mini-bootcamp, or anything similar.

Soft Skills: Often overlooked as non-critical, the soft skills section plays an essential role in illustrating your abilities as a web developer. Cater to the job description but try to go beyond the basic buzzwords.
For example, let's say the job listing included the phrase "Must function well under tight deadlines."

Typical soft skill listed in a resume: "...I work well under tight deadlines..."

Getting better: "...I thrive in deadline-based environments..."

Even better: "As the lead developer for a local magazine's website, deadline-based work culture is my default working environment."

In the third example, the candidate is not only directly addressing the requirement in the job listing; she's also giving her experience some context. You can focus on one, two, or three soft skills in this section as opposed to a shortly-worded bullet point list while taking up the same amount of vertical space.

Here's an example.

Typical soft skills section:

- Team player
- Offer constructive feedback
- Work well under tight deadlines
- Excellent communicator
- Flexible & self-motivated worker

versus a high-impact soft skills section:

- As the developer for a local magazine's website, **deadline-based work culture** is my **default working environment**.
- Collaborating with a team of twenty at a 500-capacity venue, I'm proficient in **continuous communication** while giving new hires **critical job guidance**.
- **Quick to adapt** to changing technical priorities with **minimal supervision** or guidance.

References: Not included at this stage. While you should be ready to provide references, there's really no good reason to give out personal information of references in the earliest phase of the application process.

Additional Links: The additional links consist of the two remaining clover leaves of the holy clover: Github account link and Portfolio link.

Resume Length: Notice also that Michelle's resume has been edited to one page. The cardinal rule of editing is that each word needs to be begging for its existence.

Stuffing your resume with achievements only leads to eye fatigue, more scrolling, and less focus on your main selling points as a job candidate. It becomes a distraction rather than an invitation.

Sometimes you can consolidate a two-page resume into one page by rearranging the design and layout. If you absolutely cannot edit any more information about yourself without diminishing your best qualities as a candidate, get creative with your layout. Often, this can free up some space without reducing font sizes or feeling cluttered.

Extras: Should I Include...

Personal sites? Personal websites are fine to include as long as they are somehow related to web development. Maybe you have a blog that tracks your progress as a self-taught developer. Your personal site might also double as a home for your portfolio. Maybe it's a simple landing page that describes who you are in a few short sentences. Any of these scenarios can be a great way to showcase your skills.

LinkedIn? LinkedIn links are also fine to include. Make sure they echo the most important parts of your actual resume you'll be submitting to the company.

Sometimes companies allow you to submit your LinkedIn instead of your resume. While convenient, this method doesn't allow you to customize it for individual companies. As a one-size-fits-all site, LinkedIn's real strength in this context is reinforcing your core developer skills.

Social Media? *Think carefully before including social media links.* Unless they are 100% tech-related, these accounts do little to add to your image as a web developer and worse, they are often used as tools for discrimination. While you may not have photo albums of scandals waiting to happen, company personnel aren't looking for cat memes, baby photos, political posts, or other miscellaneous materials. If they *are* interested, it's often to weed you out as a candidate.

If you decide to include your social media links, review your privacy settings so your potential employer is able to see the relevant parts of your profile.

Chapter 3

The Craft of the Cover Letter

Cover letters are a misunderstood concept in the job application process. Many applicants don't know how to construct them, or worse – don't include them at all. This is good news for you as a developer, because in this chapter we're going to go over how to craft a cover letter that inspires the reader to investigate you.

You've probably submitted cover letters before. Perhaps you've crafted one the traditional way, including things like your home address, the company's address, and a title such as "Dear Mr. Stevens" or even "To Whom it May Concern."

Flowery formalities worked fine in the old days, but times have changed. People don't need to see addresses on your cover letter. Other components that may have relevance are difficult to track down, like the exact person who is going to be reading your materials (a lot of times, it's many). And the "To Whom it May Concern" along with obvious, template-like phrases including "resume attached" only label yourself as just another candidate in the heap.

You'll need to spice it up without being gimmicky or cheesy. At the same time, you'll need to do what a cover letter is supposed to ultimately do: give the reader some reasons to look inside and investigate you further.

There are three things you should do when crafting a cover letter:

1. Introduce yourself.
2. Address the job requirements by matching them with your experience and skills.
3. Explicitly invite the reader to check out your resume (call to action).

Let's look at a cover letter that fulfills these requirements.

August 1, 2018

Hello Company X! My name is Lou, and I believe in developing beautiful and functional web applications that solve problems using the MERN stack.

I read more about your opening for a junior MERN developer and believe my professional goals align with yours: since 2016 I've been developing and designing websites and apps that are visually appealing, fast while fully-featured, and financially successful. My tech stack:

Daily Tech: HTML5, CSS3, JavaScript, jQuery, Git/GitHub
Weekly Tech: MongoDB, Express, React, Node
Monthly Tech: MySQL, Selenium WebDriver, Jekyll
Currently Learning: GraphQL, Python, Headless Chrome

I also have significant experience designing and prototyping in Photoshop, Adobe XD, and CSS. As a volunteer EMT, I work well under pressure and can expertly handle unexpected situations, whether among people or inside the code editor.

If you think we might be a good fit, please contact me at (555)-555-9871 or lou@lougriffin.com. I would love to talk more.

Thank you,

Lou Griffin

Introduction – One or two sentences to greet the reader. Despite his research, the readers' names are unknown to Lou, so he uses the company name instead.

Body – Split into three parts.

The first part gives a narrative-style description of the developer's tech specialty: the MERN stack.

The second part is split into an attention-grabbing list that details daily, weekly, monthly, and currently-learning tech. This segmented approach illustrates the candidate's core competencies, his frequency of applying secondary competencies, along with the his interest in expanding his tech stack.

The third part emphasizes "nice-to-haves" (designing and prototyping) while listing verifiable soft skills.

Conclusion & Sign-Off – Friendly wrap-up with an invitation to read his resume. Phone number and email is also included for quick contact.

Think of your cover letter as a protective cover keeping your resume, Github page, and portfolio safe from psychological dust and other debris. This gateway document leads your reader to the important things. Therefore, it's critical that you make it appetizing in your words and presentation. As with your other materials, always proofread your cover letter (read it aloud slowly or have a friend read it), check links to ensure they're live, and double-check your email address, phone, and spelling of the company name along with other proper nouns.

To summarize, you should always send a cover letter with your application materials. So many people skip this step because they believe it takes too much time to customize the content for every employer they apply to – but would you be willing to change a few nouns and invest just a few more minutes of time if it meant getting called in for an interview? Most developers would answer with a resounding yes.

Chapter 4

Gitting Good with GitHub

Simply stated, GitHub is a site where you publish your code. Each project of yours is stored inside a repository, or *repo*, where users can see your code that fuels your websites, web apps, and other coding adventures.

As you can imagine, employers are interested in seeing your GitHub because it's one of the few places on the web where you can easily share the "under the hood" components of your projects. You may be an excellent problem solver, but if the code isn't there, you greatly diminish your chances of getting hired as a web developer.

Here's what we'll cover in this chapter:

- *Getting your best projects featured on your GitHub homepage*
- *Filling in the personal information boxes for maximum impact*
- *Giving employers an accurate picture of your talents and interests*
- *Setting up working demonstrations of your projects*
- *Techniques for filling out the Contributions box*

Why GitHub is a Holy Clover Component

Sometimes employers won't ask for a GitHub link, or don't take the time to check out your projects once you submit your application materials. Don't let these possibilities prevent you from investing in a GitHub account. Remember, getting hired is a multi-step process, and there's a good chance you'll be talking about your projects and your code at interviews.

GitHub makes "show and tell" easy for developers. You might be asked to show the hiring staff some of your code on the conference room's big screen; you'll need a quick and standardized way to access this code rather than fumbling through your local computer's file directory, or worse – unable to share any code because you forgot your laptop at home. GitHub is here to save the day.

In addition, you can *fork* (copy) other users' projects to your own GitHub account, allowing you to get inspiration and even play around with the code and suggest edits — all without affecting the original project. There are many other things you can do on GitHub with an overwhelming number of options. Unfortunately, because it's easy to feature other peoples' projects while under-developing personal ones, many developers' GitHub accounts don't highlight him or her as the ideal job candidate.

No doubt, GitHub can be intimidating for new developers. Git, a version control technology that powers our interactions with GitHub, isn't as hot as the latest and greatest tech stack, so sometimes its importance is underemphasized, leaving you unable to maximize GitHub's features. The best way around that is to learn some basic Git commands and implement them when using GitHub on the command line. This is also a good skill to have because nearly all tech companies use version control, whether it's git, Mercurial, or something else.

GitHub vs. Git

So how does GitHub work with Git? Simply stated, Git allows you to issue commands that control the code your write. Git works with GitHub to keep track of your code changes and creates different versions of your files. There are many benefits to this system. For one, you can revert back to old copies of your code in case you make mistakes or don't like your newest version of the code. GitHub also serves as a central repository when you start collaborating with others on coding projects.

Both Git and GitHub are massive topics with innumerable features but for the purposes of this book, we're going to focus on a few core tasks.

If you don't have a GitHub account yet, go ahead and open one up. Branding matters (this account is largely for marketing purposes as you sell yourself to potential employers), so give thought to your username.

Your assignment: spend a day or two getting familiar with the GitHub site; study basic Git commands and concepts like *init, commit, push, pull, fork, clone*, etc; and experiment with things like pushing a project to GitHub from your local machine along with pulling and forking projects.

Your Best Work Goes Front and Center

By default, GitHub displays the most popular repositories on your front page. In other words, if you forked vuejs/vue, which has over 100,000 stars and around 15,000 forks as of this writing, that project will be on your front page. But now we're facing a problem: employers want to see *your* work, not the work of Vue's creator. Since GitHub allows a maximum of six spaces for this area, the top six most popular repos will be displayed here. That's not good news if you're forking popular projects where you haven't contributed.

We're going to fix this in three simple steps. Instead of allowing GitHub to post the default Popular repositories section, we're going to switch to Pinned repositories. This way, you can highlight **your** projects and market your talents to employers.

Here are the steps.

Step one (above): On your homepage (also known as your Profile page), click "Customize your pinned repositories."

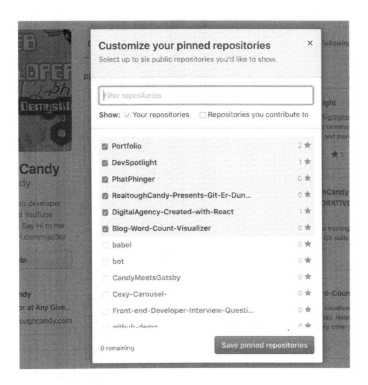

Step two: Pick up to six projects – the more you have, the better – to pin to your homepage. You have the option here of displaying projects you may have contributed to (such as a friend's or other open-source project that accepts pull requests); if you have them, consider adding one or two of these as they highlight not only your coding skills but also your teamwork and communication skills. When finished click "Save pinned repositories."

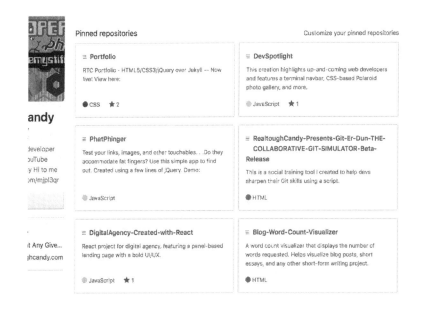

Pinned repositories   Customize your pinned repositories

⊟ Portfolio

RTC Portfolio - HTML5/CSS3/jQuery over Jekyll — Now
live! View here:

● CSS   ★ 2

⊟ DevSpotlight

This creation highlights up-and-coming web developers
and features a terminal navbar, CSS-based Polaroid
photo gallery, and more.

◌ JavaScript   ★ 1

⊟ PhatPhinger

Test your links, images, and other touchables. . .Do they
accommodate fat fingers? Use this simple app to find
out. Created using a few lines of jQuery. Demo:

◌ JavaScript

**⊟ RealtoughCandy-Presents-Git-Er-Dun-THE-
COLLABORATIVE-GIT-SIMULATOR-Beta-
Release**

This is a social training tool I created to help devs
sharpen their Git skills using a script.

● HTML

⊟ DigitalAgency-Created-with-React

React project for digital agency, featuring a panel-based
landing page with a bold UI/UX.

◌ JavaScript   ★ 1

⊟ Blog-Word-Count-Visualizer

A word count visualizer that displays the number of
words requested. Helps visualize blog posts, short
essays, and any other short-form writing project.

● HTML

Process complete. Your page now features your customized pinned repositories.

It's going to make a significant difference when employers visit your GitHub page since they now have immediate access to *your* projects. They don't have to hunt and peck for projects you've created and/or improved.

This is one of the biggest improvements you can make to your GitHub account as a job seeker. Now it's time to take the power of your projects one step further, allowing employers to see working demonstrations of your projects.

GitHub Pages and Working Demos: A Job-Seeker's Secret Weapon

One major GitHub feature that often goes unnoticed is GitHub Pages. This feature lets you turn your code into a working demo directly on GitHub, free of charge. The additional benefit of GitHub pages is that setup and deployment is *very* fast. While you won't be able to demonstrate any fullstack or backend projects (Pages supports static sites and apps only), your frontend projects can take the spotlight.

For example, let's say you developed a word-count visualizer app. This is a good candidate for GitHub Pages since it doesn't require access to a database. Here's how you'd set it up.

Push your project to GitHub like you normally do. Click on the project, and navigate to the Settings tab (above).

Scroll down to the GitHub Pages block.

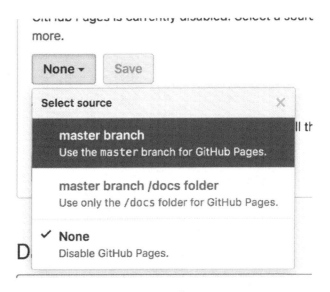

Under "Source", the default will be "None," so you will select the branch you want to feature ("master" in this case). Click save.

You'll now see the newly-created URL for your project.

GitHub Pages

GitHub Pages is designed to host your personal, organization, or project pages from a GitHub repository.

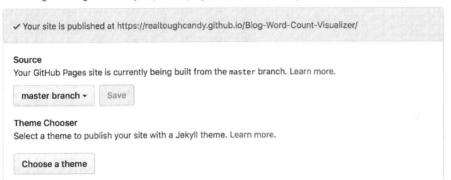

After a few minutes (sometimes longer), the page will be live. Almost done: we still need employers to see that there's actually a working demo of this project.

Copy the URL of your project's GitHub page. Navigate to the Code tab. On the right you will see the Edit button. Paste it into the Website tab.

Visitors are now able to click on your demo within the repo.

If you have fullstack projects or any other project that communicates with the backend, you'll still want to have a working demo. You can go with traditional hosting using a provider like Namecheap, upgrade to the cloud via Cloudways or Digital Ocean, you may need to deploy on Heroku, etc. Wherever you decide to host, follow the steps above to paste in the demo's URL.

Remember, this is your showcase. Dazzle these employers with your functional, fast, creative, and aesthetically-pleasing projects that have thorough descriptions.

Specifically with GitHub, *always have a working demo for each pinned project*. Fill out the description completely, and fill out the Topics section as well (located in the Edit section beneath the Code tab).

Let's now complete the personal section to reinforce yourself as a capable and motivated web developer.

Getting Personal: Profile, Bio, Profile Photo and More

There's a fine balance when it comes to sharing who you are. On one hand, who we are as developers is directly related to who we are as people. We select programming languages, tech stacks, and projects based on what motivates and fascinates us. Our learning and coding schedules are often influenced by family or other personal responsibilities. We're real people.

On the other hand, the web is a low-trust platform and we never really know who is checking out our profiles and personal details. We forget there really is such as thing as "TMI" – too much information. So what's a healthy balance? How can we share ourselves without overexposing our personal lives, yet emphasize that we're committed coders who want jobs? It's time to finesse this balancing act in GitHub's Settings area.

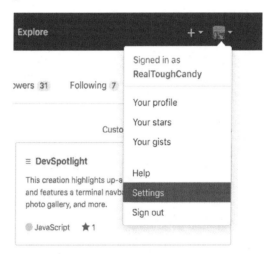

Profile. The profile section has a few options. If your account is new, the option to edit it will be on the front page. Otherwise, it's in the dropdown menu on the upper right of the page. Click Settings.

Personal settings

Profile

Account

Emails

Notifications

Billing

SSH and GPG keys

Security

Blocked users

Repositories

Organizations

Saved replies

Applications

Developer settings

Organization settings

Rockababy-
Kroppenduckel
-Industries

Public profile

Name

RealToughCandy

Public email

Select a verified email to display ⇕

You can manage verified email addresses in your email settings.

Bio

Fulltime fullstack web developer (MERN & LAMP) and YouTube webdev personality. Lover of bikes, alt rock, and cats.

You can @mention other users and organizations to link to them.

0 remaining

URL

www.realtoughcandy.com

Company

@realtoughcandy

You can @mention your company's GitHub organization to link it.

Location

Near a Text Editor at Any Given Moment

All of the fields on this page are optional and can be deleted at any time, and by filling them out, you're giving us consent to share this data wherever your user profile appears. Please see our privacy statement to learn more about how we use this information.

Update profile

Profile picture

Upload new picture

Fill out as much as possible. You may list your specific location or just give a general idea to where you're located (location discrimination is a reality, even if you're open to relocation).

The Bio section, located on the Profile page above, should be a few words to confirm you're the person you've told your potential employers about. You've seen the classic example: "Web Developer. React aficionado. Hiker. Cat lover." While this technique is employed by many, it does a good job of quickly summarizing you.

Profile picture. Github will assign a default "identicon" to your profile if Gravatar (a service that provides avatars) can't find a photo associated with your email. In either situation, have a picture that represents you as a developer. It doesn't necessarily need to be a selfie. If you're trying to minimize your chances of pre-interview age (or other) discrimination, you can go with a tech-themed icon.

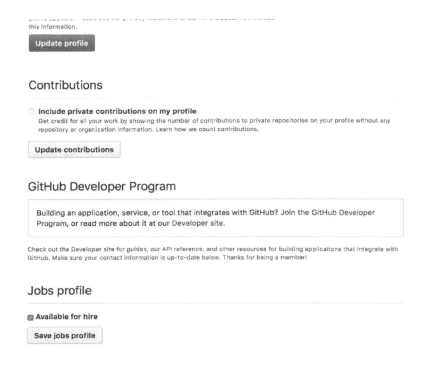

Beneath the **Update profile** button, there is a Jobs profile (above). Check the box to notify the public that you're available for hire.

Ghost Town or Gold Rush? The Contributions Box

There is one additional component that needs your attention: the contributions box. This is a visual map of the days and frequency of your GitHub contributions. In other words, GitHub records every time you make a commit or pull request (with some restrictions) and inserts that record into your contributions box.

1,584 contributions in the last year

Contribution activity   Jump to ▾   2018

June 2018

⬚ Created 80 commits in 11 repositories   ⚑

2017

2016

2015

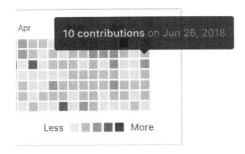

A contributions box with little activity is not a good sign for potential employers. On the other hand, a contributions box with many shaded squares means you're an active developer who cares about committing your code, refactoring your code, adding new personal projects to your profile, and contributing to open-source projects other than your own.

If your contributions box is looking largely shaded, you can probably skip over the rest of this section. However, if there are chunks of gray on your profile, or you don't know what else you can do to get those contributions numbers up, you'll need to start taking action to irrigate this GitHub contribution desert.

Rocking the Docs

There's a quick, easy way to add to your contributions: **documentation**. Go over your projects and start commenting sections of code that need explanation. In addition, you can also edit your README file (the file that tells people what your project is all about, how to use it, etc.). Most READMEs can always use improvements or further explanation and this is a fine way to bump up your contribution numbers.

These quick tweaks are counted in addition to any changes you make to your actual codebase, and every contribution has equal weight. So, whether you commit a whole new feature to your web app, simply fix some spacing issues, or correct a grammatical error in the README, each commit counts as a single contribution.

You don't have to be on GitHub at every waking hour doing things, but you should make a point to visit and contribute throughout the week to maintain consistency. Even a five-minute visit can make a significant difference.

Final Review

The final step in the GitHub improvement process should be to proofread and test the features you want your employers to see. Have a friend navigate and test the site, too – an extra pair of eyes is invaluable in the proofreading process.

Now that we've weaponized our GitHub account so that employers can't resist, it's time to do the same thing to our portfolio.

Chapter 5

Polishing Your Portfolio

If your resume and cover letter is where you're telling, your Github and Portfolio is where you're showing. It's time to start exhibiting your capabilities, interests, and knowledge.

As in other career fields like graphic design, a portfolio is a collection of your best work. Before the web, prospective employees would often carry in a physical portfolio of their work, showing off each piece. The interviewer(s) would ask questions about it. The interviewee would answer those questions while highlighting particular achievements and techniques used in each creation. The ultimate goal was to make the interviewer say, "Well! That's some good stuff, isn't it? I want you to do something like that for *our* company."

This is the same effect we want to have with our online web development portfolio. Just as the best old-school graphic artists brought in their best work on clean, crisp paper inside a fresh folder, so must we in the digital sphere.

Here's what we'll cover in this chapter:

- *Setting up your portfolio for maximum impact*
- *What projects to include*
- *Giving your projects context*
- *Showing employers you know how to make smart technical decisions*

It's easy to feel self-doubt over a portfolio, especially when you start getting deep into analyzing your work. Have any of these self-doubting quips ever popped into your head?

"Do companies even want to see this project? All the projects I see online are so much better."

"A million other people have this project in their portfolio."

"Nobody uses this kind of project in the real world."

We're going to go over these scenarios further in this chapter because they are common concerns with developers. However – as you'll see shortly – they *can* be resolved using some creative thinking and problem-solving techniques.

First, let's go over how to set up your portfolio.

This is your portfolio and nobody else's – it's a good feeling! You've worked hard to develop interesting projects and now it's time to go public. No two portfolios will look alike.

There's no recommended or standardized platform for web developer portfolios – you can code something from scratch; use CSS frameworks like Bootstrap or Skeleton; customize (or create) a WordPress theme; you can even use something like a static site generator such as Jekyll or Gatsby.

Your portfolio is a project in itself so if you choose a pre-built theme, give it some customization. This is also a learning experience so it's fine if it takes you a few weeks to get it up and running. A good first step to creating your portfolio is to assess the needs of your user:

- Like all users, employers want the site to be fast. Select a reputable web hosting provider and choose a tech stack that isn't tarnished with slow performance. Compress images. If you're using WordPress, use the absolute bare essentials for plugins.

- Employers are looking at many portfolios so remind them who created yours. You could arrange your name and title (frontend developer, etc.) somewhere on the header or have a hero image with some text. You'll also want to include a contact form. Test this feature before going live to ensure messages are getting to you.

- Make your navigation simple. Some developers use a one-page design that starts with an introduction, transitions into a skills section, then sails into their portfolio. This way, the developer efficiently controls the flow of information.

- Themes save time and lead to better user experiences. A Google search will provide results for free options for whatever platform you choose. Themes, and especially WordPress themes, often have the benefit of being responsive and multiple-browser supported right out of the box. While you'll still want to do some testing, you don't have to worry about investing days of your time creating and troubleshooting separate experiences for users. As mentioned, tweak the theme to match your style.

- Your domain name should be easy to remember and spell.

Now that you understand the technical components of your portfolio, let's explore the content you'll include.

Projects are the Protein of Your Portfolio

Projects are the protein of your portfolio; the meat. You'll need to have an intimate understanding of what problems they solve and why you coded what you coded. This is the place where your skills are truly tested. It's not just about whether you can code or not – it's about how well you make decisions and understand the impact of those decisions.

The first decision you need to make is what projects go into the portfolio. The simple answer: **strictly your best ones.** And by best, this means the **projects that solve a problem**.

You also need to assess what kind of company you want to work for. Will this company be an ecommerce or possibly WordPress shop? If so, feature projects with PHP and shopping cart features, and any plugins or themes you've developed. Or maybe you see yourself at a startup that uses only the hottest new frontend frameworks: highlight your work with React, Angular, or Vue. You may have done some killer work on a legacy project that uses an esoteric language, but companies want to see projects that reflect *their* tech stack.

Let's say you want to work for a company that develops with React. You have three solid projects in that framework along with two vanilla JavaScript apps. Should you still publish your portfolio with all of these? **Absolutely**. React is built on vanilla (plain) JavaScript and developers need to have a grasp of the fundamentals of the language to truly understand how frontend frameworks operate. Whether it's PHP, JavaScript, Python, Ruby, or anything else, any projects of yours that utilize a framework's underlying language are appropriate to include in portfolios—assuming your ideal job requires knowledge of a framework.

How Many Projects Should I Include?

Now that you know what to include, you'll need to decide how much of it to include. There are no standard minimums or maximums, but you'll risk underwhelming employers if you have only two or three projects, and most likely overwhelm them if they have to pick from more than six or seven. A happy, manageable number is five to six. This way, you can include projects from multiple domains like paying clients, personal projects, and open-source contributions. Plus, when it's limited to five or six, you won't be struggling to remember which project your employer casually mentions when it's interview time.

After developers decide on what projects to choose, their final act will be adding a few screenshots and linking to the live site. This is where you're given a huge advantage over those applicants because you're going to give your projects some much-needed context.

Getting on Par with PSR/PAR

Often, creative agencies will show off their client work by implementing something called a case study. Case studies sound academic, but what they essentially do is explain to the reader why the team made the choices they did. What was the team's problem and their goals; what was their *process*? The case study format is an excellent vehicle for delivering context to projects, but sometimes it can be hard to execute. Additionally, the case study format makes it easy for developers to include too much information, risking losing readers' interest.

A more modular and focused format web developers should use is problem/solution/result (PSR). Sometimes this method is also called problem/action/result (PAR). Whatever you choose to call it, remember that it's a potent tool when it comes to your portfolio. PSRs allow you to quickly extract and explain the relevance of your projects. Let's break it down.

Problem – What problem needed to be solved?

Solution – What actions did you take to solve this problem?

Result – What was the outcome of your project? In other words, what happened as a result of your actions?

You should implement a PSR structure for each of your portfolio projects.

In the following example, the PSR has been changed to CSO (challenge/solution/outcome), but the acronyms mean the same thing.

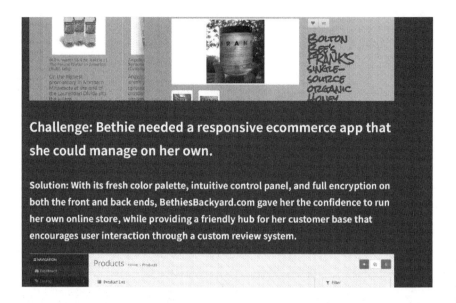

Challenge: Bethie needed a responsive ecommerce app that she could manage on her own.

Solution: With its fresh color palette, intuitive control panel, and full encryption on both the front and back ends, BethiesBackyard.com gave her the confidence to run her own online store, while providing a friendly hub for her customer base that encourages user interaction through a custom review system.

In addition to the PSR statement, this developer included relevant screenshots as well as links to the live site. Although not shown in here, you could also link to the Github repo.

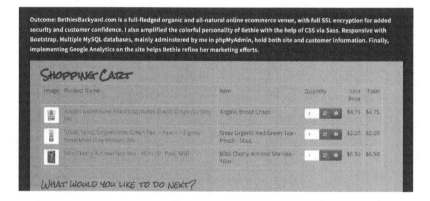

These components create a cohesive and compelling project package.

Isn't it so much better than only a screenshot and a project title? Employers definitely think so.

Bethie's checkout page is simple, roomy, and secure.

Stylin' and Profilin'

We've got the protein of our portfolio installed, the portfolio site itself looks good and is fully functional, and there is context given to each project for maximum impact. It's time to do a final pass ensuring that:

- All copy is free of grammatical and spelling errors. Punctuation is used appropriately.
- Images and other media are compressed.
- Colors, fonts, and other styling used on your portfolio match or complement the styling used on your other application materials.
- Your contact page/form is functional. Email is delivered to an address you check regularly. Any phone numbers listed are in service.
- All links are live and functional.
- The site is responsive.
- You've read your PSRs aloud (or had a friend proofread them) and they flow well.

If you passed this final checklist, you're ready to bundle your holy clover application materials and start applying for jobs. It's a great feeling, but some developers still may have some doubts about their projects. To close this chapter, let's go over a few self-doubting inner dialogues that creep into the minds of many developers.

Self-Doubts

"Do companies even want to see this project? All the projects I see online are so much better."

Employers want to see projects that solve a problem. It can be a common problem, an esoteric problem, a theoretical problem – the type of problem is irrelevant in this situation. However, the issue with including things like TODO lists is that while they **do** solve a problem, that problem has already been solved a million times or more. Every web developer has created a TODO list – sometimes multiple!

Does your TODO do something better or more efficiently? Only then will it have a competitive advantage, just like in the real world. So, it's not that companies don't want to see your TODO list, Facebook clone, or color picker app. It's just that these types of projects have been tackled many times before. Unless you can bring a fresh twist to an old standard, leave it out.

As far as online projects you see being so much better – it can be discouraging. But remember, these kinds of projects are often built by very experienced developers, a team of developers, or geniuses destined for greatness. The fastest path to hopelessness in web development is to compare yourself to child prodigies who code quadratic formula calculators in their sleep. Try to steer your thoughts and emotions towards something more productive. The only person you should be comparing yourself to is yourself: your last year's self, your last month's self, even your yesterday's self.

"A million other people have this project in their portfolio."

As noted, it's not good to include super-popular projects like TODO lists in your portfolio because everybody does them. However, there's a way around this: add a feature to it. What about a quick-share function that allows third parties to view it, like a spouse or co-worker? Or a way to save your TODO for tomorrow, even if you close your browser? Give it a twist.

"Nobody uses this kind of project in the real world."

Maybe not, but how do you know for sure? Impractical or theoretical projects often lead to brilliant real-life implementations down the road. These projects deserve inclusion in your portfolio. It bears repeating: *if the project solves a problem, employers want to see it.* They *really* want to see it if it's unique and you're able to convey its value (even if theoretical).

You've created and edited your resume, cover letter, GitHub account, and portfolio, and things are starting to shine. Now, it's time to start looking for jobs and getting this information to the right people.

Chapter 6

Finding a Job

Locating appropriate jobs takes time, effort, and patience. Your eyes will glaze over, your head might start hurting, but once you develop a method for locating jobs, the application process will be much smoother.

First, read over Appendix B for quality job listing sites. There are too many sites online that don't have jobs for junior developers or are just plain bogus – these are huge time sinks.

Second, do your research. If you've dedicated your development journey to PHP and your city of choice doesn't have many PHP positions, you may need to expand your search. Relocation is expensive; start saving as much money as you can. Additionally, ask if the company offers a relocation allowance when you interview with them.

Now, prepare a filter list. Write down all the basic requirements you need in a web developer job. For example:

- Open to relocation but prefer Portland
- LAMP stack
- Full time (40 hrs/wk)
- No huge corporations

You can use the sites' filtering system for some of these requirements, such as distance-based location results, but others will need to be manually sorted. One way of doing this efficiently on many sites is to use their built-in filtering system for the basics, then opt to receive daily email updates that include those listings. Bookmark all positions in that email that interest you (you'll see why shortly).

Requirements: Reality vs. Expectations

While there are thousands of unfilled positions for junior developer jobs at this very moment, many job listings don't use "junior" as a keyword. And even if they do, a lot of times these listings aren't written by developers, but by people in human resources. Have you ever seen a job listing that said the company was looking for a modern web developer to build progressive web apps, but needed to have five years of experience in Java and Python, along with years of experience in outdated tech like SOAP? It was probably written by a human resources specialist outside the tech department. That might be an extreme example, but when you see a job listing that mostly fits your tech stack and says "3+ years experience," **apply anyway.** When you see "Bachelor's Degree in Computer Science" and you don't have that, **apply anyway.** When you see a list of "nice-to-haves" of tech you aren't familiar with, **apply anyway.**

Never let their "nice-to-haves" list stop you from applying. This is a wish list—a fantasy call to the ultra-rare developers out there who can code, design, prototype, manage teams, and do whatever else. There aren't many out there and odds are, if they *can* do all those things, they're not looking at a web developer job like this in the first place.

Expanding Your Job Search via Networking

While online job boards like Indeed and the career section on Stack Overflow will provide you with thousands of web developer job listings, there are still a few other venues where you can not only generate potential leads – but establish some *really* good ones. Why? Because the best job openings are never listed. Once you start expanding beyond the traditional online job boards, you start building an invaluable network of both online and offline connections. These connections can put you in the interview chair and beyond.

Meetups

Web developer Meetups are one of the best places to start getting connected with those in the industry. Meetups, which are organized via Meetup.com, allow people to schedule events where people with similar interests can hang out, build community, and learn a thing or two. From JavaScript fans, to backend developers, down to niche gatherings of Vue enthusiasts, Meetups are diverse. Usually, the Meetups will include a featured speaker, but not before a gathering period often accompanied by (free) food and beverages. Meetups are fun and educational, and because developers are misunderstood outside the tech world, many are eager to talk to fellow devs.

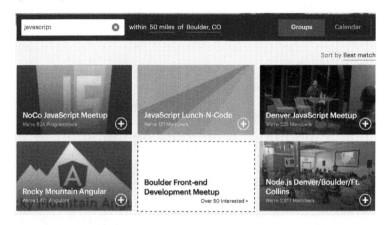

When you sign up to attend your first Meetup, one of the easiest ways to break the ice and lessen the anxiety of going to an event where you don't know anybody is to contact the organizer. This can be easily done via the Meetup page using their messaging feature. Introduce yourself, tell them you're new, and make small but genuine talk. Maybe you have a question about the event that wasn't detailed anywhere. By doing this, you already have an "in" at the Meetup and you'll have a familiar face to look forward to.

Plus, this is the person who scheduled the tech event outside her work schedule: in this woman's world, tech is more than just a day job. She knows a *lot* of developers. She likely also knows of at least a few companies who are looking for people. Make friends with this person and definitely introduce yourself at the Meetup! Give her a little bit of your backstory, and don't be shy about letting her know you're searching for a job.

This goes for anybody you might meet at the Meetup. Are they new developers, too? This person might make a great study partner or be an understanding person to talk with about your coding journey. Are they mid-to-senior-level? Maybe they're willing to become your tech mentor or have job leads as well. Meetups are filled with talented, welcoming, and motivated techies, so take advantage of these free opportunities.

Link Up with LinkedIn

LinkedIn is the go-to site for professional online networking. You don't need a profile to land a web development job but it can really help put you ahead of the competition. Much like Meetups, the LinkedIn environment is filled with web developers and, perhaps more importantly, tech recruiters.

Recruiters are responsible for finding quality talent to present to tech companies. Some are pushy; some can be unreliable; some are fantastic. Once you complete your LinkedIn profile, expect the recruiter emails to come soon thereafter. Many if not most of them will be spam but be sure to follow up with the legitimate ones – even if you don't think you're eligible. Many (if not most) times, job requirements are flexible.

Your main function on LinkedIn at this stage as a junior developer is to get noticed. You can do this in a few different ways but for maximum effect, take care of all of these components:

- Fill out your profile completely (100%).
- Make at least 50 industry-related connections (remember those Meetups you went to the other week along with the connections you made on the freeCodeCamp discussion board?).
- The education section should also include any online certificates you've earned or coding bootcamps you've attended.
- Link to your portfolio and GitHub (you can even attach photos of your projects to spice things up).
- Hoist your development-related experience to the top of the Experience box, rather than your current job that may be outside the tech industry.
- Trigger the LinkedIn algorithm by including keywords belonging to your area of expertise, peppered throughout your profile. Namedrop your tech stack(s) wherever you can without being excessive or sounding unnatural.
- Push recruiters to the next level by inviting them to contact you or requesting that they check out your portfolio or Github.

Recruiters can be an *excellent* way to get connected with job opportunities, but they don't necessarily make getting into the company any easier. Even if one contacts you and wants to move forward, your application materials will still be provided to the company he or she is representing. If chosen to move forward you will also still need to go through the interview process. Keep this in mind as the weeks progress and update your materials as your skills improve.

Discussion Boards & Social Media

As a junior developer, there's a good chance you've tried out one of the numerous online coding education platforms. Team Treehouse, Codecademy, freeCodeCamp, and many others also include a community-based forum for aspiring developers. Don't just lurk on these boards – assert yourself! Help others where you can with their questions, ask questions of your own, and fill out your profile noting your tech stack, Github/portfolio/LinkedIn links, and that you're seeking employment as a web developer. You can even add a line to your signature block in the forums, something like "Now getting hired."

Many people read these forums and you never know who might drop by with a job connection. Be sure you're easy to get ahold of – don't make people search for your email address. You want to be as contactable as possible when it comes to strangers with job leads.

In addition to maximizing your forum activities, you can also maximize your social media presence by going "full tech." For example, start retweeting developer Tweets you like, follow web developers who are interested in the frameworks and languages you enjoy (including big names like Evan You and Dan Abramov), and be courageous in mentioning that you're ready to start your career in web development.

Twitter is especially good for this since your tags can be seen by people outside your social circle. In addition, keeping your social media accounts tech-focused will help portray a professional image of you when your employer Googles your name. It's much better to have recent posts that debate the merits of PHP versus Node rather than unflattering, divisive, or politically-related posts and photos.

Deployment Day: Bombs Away

Finally, apply to at least 15 jobs a week on the same day: Deployment Day. A dedicated day gives you some time to research these companies, and you can trim off the job openings that aren't appealing to you anymore.

To spread out the workload, prep your materials earlier in the week – customize names, change your cover letter dates, organize into individual folders, and so on. This way, on Deployment Day, you can click on your saved job bookmarks, navigate to the appropriate folder on your machine, and upload efficiently. You'll learn more about the payoff of Deployment Day in Chapter 10 – salary negotiation.

Chapter 7

The Post-Application Process

In this section (Chapters 7-11), we're going to cover:

- *How to keep track of the jobs you applied to*
- *How and when to send an email check-in*
- *What to expect when companies reach out to you*
- *Interview setup and preparation*
- *The STAR interview method*
- *Tips for coding challenges/interviews*
- *How to follow up*
- *Job offers and salary negotiation*
- *Your first week on the job*

Spreading Joy with Spreadsheets

Most developers apply for a lot of jobs. Like, *a lot* a lot. This is especially true if you're a junior developer. Ask around, and it's not uncommon for developers to tell you they applied to fifty, sixty, and sometimes even *more* job openings before they secured their current position. That's a lot of time searching and applying for jobs. It's also nearly impossible to remember all of them. What happens if you get a call or an email from a company that doesn't sound familiar? Are they scammers, or did you legitimately apply?

Create a spreadsheet. Make seven columns and title them *Company Name, Date Applied, Like (1-4), Stage, Point of Contact, Job, and Location.* Every time you apply to a job, the minute you hit that submit button, open this file and fill out as much information as possible. This sheet is going to be your primary document as you start applying to more and more jobs. You are quickly able to see the summary of the jobs, and you can start prioritizing them using their likeability factor. This spreadsheet has the advantage of unloading information from your brain and onto something more concrete and manageable, which means more head space, greater accuracy, and less stress.

	A	B	C	D	E	F	G
				Web Dev Application Statuses			
2	Company Name	Date Applied	Like (1-4)	Stage (Applied/ Phone Hello/Phone Tech/On Site/ Offered	Point of Contact	Job	Location
3	RUForReal.com	Dec 22	2	Applied'		Dev	Edina, MN
4	Reggett & Blatt	Dec 22	4	Phone Hello		UX/UI	Kansas City
5	Beyfath	Dec 22	1	Applied		Web Dev	Lexena
6	JoeChimney.com	Dec 22	3	Applied	Raul	Frontend Dev	Leawood, KS
7	Rocky Paths Inc	Dec 22	3	Applied	Tina	Dev	KCMO
8	Banjanono	Dec 22	3	Phone Tech	Mr Tomi Fezri	UX	KS
9	AevCompany.com	Dec 22	3	Applied	State	Front end dev	KCMO
10	ArtisanVan	Dec 22	2	Applied	Ben	web developer	rural michigan
11	Herman Piller	Dec 22	1	Phone Hello	Chauncey	Front End Dev	Detroit
12	Software Etc	Dec 28	4	Applied		Web Dev	SIOUX FALLS SD
13	Big Poppa Education Services	Dec 28	4	On site		Web dev instructor	Northwestern (IL), NH, and KS
14	clickbait.com	Dec 28	4	Applied'	Dev	Web Dev	Urbana IA
15							
16							
17							
18	Avoid:	ScamLicity.com					
19	REJECTEDS						
20	Whizbobo	DID NOT HEAR BACK September					
21	chocorama.com	DID NOT HEAR BACK September					
22	EventPunk	Not a good fit					

A tracker's usefulness increases as you submit your applications.

This document is dynamic. You'll find yourself updating information as the days go by, ranging from fluctuating likeability scores to the stage of the application process. Did you find out some juicy details about the company and its work culture that changes your perception of them? Get a call from a hiring manager? Update the spreadsheet. Often there will be employers that you disqualify because you changed your mind or weren't selected to move forward in the application process. It's a good idea to put those listings outside of the 'live' area but still accessible for record keeping.

Help, They're Not Emailing Me

For every minute that goes by when you're waiting for a response, it seems like an eternity. In the meantime, continue searching for jobs and prepping your materials for your next application deployment day. Continue to build your technical skills and consider writing a "check-in" email. This last component can be particularly useful when you want to plant a seed in the company's collective mind that you're motivated and assertive – qualities that companies love.

The Check-In

A check-in email is like a follow-up email, but it takes a more proactive yet general approach. Whereas a follow-up is meant for specific people after a personal interaction, a check-in is sent to strangers prior to any personal interaction.

Let's say you applied for a frontend developer job. You read the job posting but nowhere did it say when the job application period closed. It could close today, it could be next year; it may even be one of those evergreen listings where companies are always collecting applications for a future hiring period.

It's been a week since you submitted your materials and you've only received one email since then – the auto-generated application confirmation. At this point, after seven days or so (but not earlier), you would start crafting your check-in.

Here's how to do it: find the point of contact for the job on your spreadsheet. If you don't have one, go to the company's website and look for their human resources department. If you still can't find it, use their general inquiry address. Many times, this starts with a "hello@" followed by the company's domain name.

Write something like this (customize to fit your personality but keep it professional):

Hi weWantVueDevs,

Robin O'Bryan here. I applied to your frontend web developer opening recently and just wanted to check in with you to express my continued interest in the position.

Is there a timeline I can expect for the first round of candidate callbacks/interviews? Thanks for your time and looking forward to talking soon!

Robin

Don't make yourself look overly-motivated or even desperate by writing a check-in email before this seven-day timeline. Even smaller companies have a lot going on and you'll risk coming across as that pushy candidate who needs extra attention. Play it cool.

The Callback/Emailback

You wake up on a typical weekday and do what you always do first thing: check your email. Between yet another unsolicited pizza coupon, spam from strangers making even stranger promises, and social media alerts notifying you that your bestie from high school just walked outside, you see a message from a familiar organization with a subject line of "Web Developer Position."

There are two potential messages contained in this email.

First: "Thank you for applying. We received many applications and it was hard to choose, but we will not be proceeding with your application at this time."

Second: "We were really impressed with what we saw. When are you available to meet?"

If you receive a rejection email, **don't let it depress you. Keep searching for jobs.** No doubt, you're going to get a few of these types of emails, especially once you start applying to 40, 50, 60, and even 70 or more jobs. Even if you're perfectly qualified, you'll still end up getting some "Thanks, but no thanks" emails. It's disappointing, but it's nothing personal: *you just have to keep searching for and applying to more jobs.*

But what happens when you get an email of the *second* variety? No gimmicks this time – they want to talk with you! This isn't a big deal; this is a *huge* deal. Why? Because something about you piqued the interest of the people responsible for hiring web developers.

They're curious about you.

They want to see if you're the same person in real life as you are in your application materials.

They're ready for the next step.

The emailback (some organizations still use phone calls for their first outreach) is an email from a representative of the company that expresses their interest in learning more about you. The tone of the message may be informal ("Hey Stef!"), but make no mistake, underneath the casual veneer is all business.

Emailbacks are sent for one thing: establishing a date, time, and place to talk more. Some organizations require a brief phone screen followed by multiple rounds of interviews on different days; others have no phone screen and one big day of interviews, but whatever the configuration, this first meeting is critical.

As mentioned, many times the tone of the email will be casual, especially in the case of startups. Don't make the mistake of mirroring that person's tone – you can be a bit more casual with words once you build rapport and get to know people. As with your other written communication like your email check-in, keep it direct but friendly.

Here is an example of a reply to an emailback:

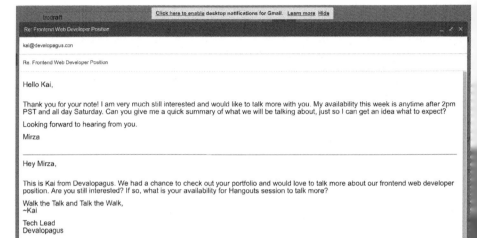

Hello Kai,

Thank you for your note! I am very much still interested and would like to talk more with you. My availability this week is anytime after 2pm PST and all day Saturday. Can you give me a quick summary of what we will be talking about, just so I can get an idea what to expect?

Looking forward to hearing from you.

Mirza

Hey Mirza,

This is Kai from Devalopagus. We had a chance to check out your portfolio and would love to talk more about our frontend web developer position. Are you still interested? If so, what is your availability for Hangouts session to talk more?

Walk the Talk and Talk the Walk,
~Kai

Tech Lead
Devalopagus

Note that the tech lead used the word "talk." While sometimes it means just that, most times it is used as an informal word to mean "interview." Either way, this conversation will establish the first impression, setting much of the tone for the rest of your interview journey. Mirza acted smart and asked upfront for details on what to expect. He also made sure to specify his timezone since unanticipated time differences are a major cause of disaster.

Chapter 8

The Interviews

It's not a typo – the typical hiring process for web developers, even juniors, involves more than one interview. Further, these interviews can vary in style, starting with a phone screen and evolving to the all-day, on-site rounds of interviews where you will be challenged technically, mentally, physically, and emotionally. In this chapter we're going to look at the types of interviews you may encounter along with how to handle yourself when engaging with people from the company.

As mentioned earlier, employers ultimately want employees to do two things

1. Make the business money.
2. Save the business money.

Every employee action can be related back to one or both of these objectives. For example, is the employee a clean coder? She just saved and made the company money by clearly and concisely commenting her code so future developers can read it easily and code faster. Is she a good communicator? Her style of communication is easy for people to understand, so when she gives directives there aren't misunderstandings – as a result, actions are completed more efficiently.

Now, look at this scenario from the opposite side: is the employee a sloppy coder? She cost the company a lot of money because future developers don't understand her code, wasting thousands of hours of manpower. Is she a poor communicator? Her co-workers don't enjoy working with her, which certainly takes a toll on output (not to mention office morale – this person may even motivate some co-workers to look for another employer).

Ultimately, if you can convince the interviewers that you can make them money and/or save them money, along with proving you're a regular human being rather than an emotionless cyborg, you have a *really* good chance at getting that job.

But how do you do that level of convincing? For this, we're going to use the STAR method.

The STAR Interview Method

Remember how you refactored your portfolio using the PSR/PAR method? We're going to apply a similar method in our interviews. STAR stands for Situation→ Task → Action → Results. The STAR method allows you to quickly organize your answer while succinctly describing the process you used to solve a problem. In this industry, processes are important.

The STAR method, step-by-step:

1. **S is for Situation.** Describe the situation.
-Your interviewer wants to know the specific scenario and challenge you faced.
-Keep the situation related to web development so that it's relevant to the job position.

2. **T is for Task.** How did you approach the situation?
-In this step, you share what your plan was for solving the problem. Be descriptive.

3. **A is for Action.** What actionable steps did you take?
-Your interviewer wants to know your role in solving the problem.
-Tell the interviewer what you did to implement the solution.

4. **R is for Result.** What was the outcome of your solution?
-What measurable effects did your solution have?

S Situation	Detail the background. Provide a context. Where? When?
T Task	Describe the challenge and expectations. What needed to be done? Why?
A Action	Elaborate your specific action. What did you do? How? What tools did you use?
R Results	Explain the results: accomplishments, recognition, savings, etc. Quantify.

The STAR method lets you build value with your words.

Let's apply this method to a common scenario: you're in an interview, and your interviewer asks you an open-ended question about new tech: "What new technologies have you been using lately?"

Many candidates don't see the nuances of a question like this and answer with something like, "I've really been enjoying React because the virtual DOM is cool." Or, "I just started playing around with GraphQL on a project and it's awesome!"

This isn't helpful for the interviewer and not really what they're looking for. Sure, you enjoy GraphQL – but so what? Here's what:

"**(Situation)** I was recently working for an ecommerce client and I noticed I was interacting with and writing a lot of low-level data access code.
(Task) I knew I needed a better solution to deal with all the data because it was really inefficient. I read more about GraphQL and its simplicity is brilliant. The backend stability, the elegant data retrieval, the way it reduces bottlenecks between different servers really put it over the edge as I researched other options.
(Action) I consulted with my client about doing some enhancements to their code base and they agreed. I wrapped their RESTful API in GraphQL and within a few days we were ready to go.
(Result) The requester now gets a single entry point which is huge for query efficiency and load times. From a labor standpoint, this transition has freed at least six hour a week since I'm no longer troubleshooting a massive amount of API calls when things go wrong. Tests have even shown some queries to load up to two seconds faster for users.
(You being human and not a cyborg) So yeah, GraphQL has been pretty awesome and I just love the efficiency it offers."

Most people wouldn't be able to smoothly and naturally relate the above – that's a lot to say! Further, delivering long blocks of verbal information without taking a few pauses just sounds weird. And it's OK to show emotions or be emphatic here; this is your life and livelihood. Be less concerned with the structure of your sentences, more concerned about sharing a narrative using the STAR method. STAR is the skeleton that shapes your compelling story.

A final note on STAR: Not all questions are appropriate for this method. For example, questions about algorithms, design patterns, and programming principles are purely technical in nature and don't require a narrative. STAR is best applied to open-ended questions.

Types of Interview Questions

Here are some common topics you are likely to encounter. These will vary depending on your stack:

- **Behavioral questions** (Can be technical: "Company A is considering a massive SEO-driven overhaul on their site. What questions do you ask them from a web developer standpoint?" Can also be soft-skills related: "Your co-worker is telling you that he took company code and started selling it on an online marketplace because according to him, the company isn't paying him what he's worth. What do you do?" Behavioral questions are perfect for using the STAR method.)
- **Algorithms**
- **Programming principles**
- **OO design patterns**
- **Experience with the company's tech stack**
- **Familiarity with current tech** (open-ended questions such as "Tell me about what new tech you've been using.")
- **Deep dive into your portfolio**, possibly a code review on select projects
- **"Trivia" tech** ("What is the difference between double- and triple-equal signs in JavaScript?")
- **You** (Be prepared to talk about yourself!)

Oral technical interviews are tough by default. When was the last time somebody asked you about JavaScript scope and you explained it, verbally, on the spot? Try and practice with a friend or family member and have them ask you some questions found in the resources listed in Appendix A. This will help get you accustomed to answering questions using technical language in a low-pressure atmosphere where you're free to make mistakes and finesse your delivery.

Coding Challenges

You may also be given a coding challenge. However, unlike those terrifying videos you see on YouTube, most junior developers won't be asked to use a whiteboard to solve data structure problems or dive into the theory behind Big O notation. Those are usually reserved for software engineers (a different career path), and senior ones at that. More likely, if you *are* given a coding challenge, it will be on a computer in front of the interviewer(s), or as a "take-home" assignment to be completed by a specified time.

The exact coding challenge varies by company, but consider it nothing more than a test: while the problem may be challenging, it's designed to assess your skills.

You may be tasked to recreate a website.

You might be given a list of two or three coding "brain-teasers" that involve turning word problems into code or further fleshed out as an actual app.

You may be tasked to refactor bad code.

For take-home assignments, remember that you have the world at your command. It's not cheating to reach out for help – developers do it every day with Google when they get stuck on a problem. If you get stuck, do some Google'ing, schedule a meeting with your tech mentor, or even take a walk or meditate on the coding challenge. Break the problem down into smaller, manageable pieces. Your coding challenge *is* solvable no matter how foreign it may look at first glance.

While take-home coding challenges are popular for junior developers, companies sometimes do opt for real-time coding interviews. You may be asked to write original code, debug preexisting code, or answer coding questions. Just like with the take-home coding challenges – this is a test. But in this test, the interviewers want to see your *process,* so **be verbal when you're coding**. **Think aloud.** This is *so* critical.

Put another way: *explain your thought process and justify your choices as you solve the problem*. Even if you can't solve the problem, the way you explain your process is more important than getting the answer correct.

Here are some more pointers:

- Confirm that everybody is on the same page before you start coding: ask your interviewer any questions about your assumptions.
- Use the appropriate technical terms and formal names.
- Use semantic naming conventions (i.e. var multiply_numbers instead of var x).

Interviewing The Company

So far, all of this information has been from the perspective of you in the interview chair. But remember, you also get to put *your* interviewer in that chair. Employment is a two-way street and you want to make sure this job is aligned with your personal and professional goals. Be sure you're receiving clear information on the job position, and feel free to ask them questions like:

- What's the company culture like?
- Do you have a formal training process? Who will be my lead(s)?
- What's the workflow like?
- What's the day in the life of a typical junior developer like?
- What are my daily responsibilities?
- What developer tools do your devs currently use?
- What OS does this shop run on? What OSes do our clients run on?
- Do you adhere to coding standards (i.e. PHP's PSR, company standard, etc.)?
- What do you offer in terms of continuing education and career advancement?

Bring a notebook and pens to these interviews and be prepared to write lots of notes.

Interview Environments

Whether it's a simple "How early can you be here tomorrow?" or a not-so-simple calendar app to schedule a 90-minute Skype session with a core crew of developers halfway around the world, interview environments vary among employers.

Here are some common configurations:

- Phone screen→realtime video (Skype, Google Hangouts, etc.)→in-person→decision
- Phone screen→in-person→decision
- Realtime video screen→technical phone interview→decision
- Realtime video→in-person→decision
- Realtime video→decision
- In-person→decision

The list goes on, but each environment warrants its own preparation. A phone or video screen is exactly how it sounds: used to "screen" the best candidates from the rest of the pack.

Try to map out the sequence before going live to each of these environments. For example, if you're scheduled for a realtime video interview:

- Find a quiet place in your home with a strong Wi-Fi signal. Use an ethernet cable if necessary.
- Use a laptop or desktop rather than a smartphone.
- Choose a background with minimal distractions.
- Ensure the lighting is ample and illuminates you well.
- Video conference apps are power hogs. Keep the power supply plugged in to your laptop. This will also reduce fan noise.
- Ensure your camera and microphone are operational.
- Consider doing a "dry run" with a friend or family member.
- **Absolutely have a backup plan.** Internet crashes, browser incompatibility issues and cameras and mics that suddenly stop working are disaster situations.

Back it Up

The last bullet point also applies to mobile devices when you're on a phone call. Dead zones, low battery life, and lagging connections are just as toxic for your personal success as video problems. Back that thing up and have a plan B.

In-person interviews warrant preparation as far as logistics are concerned. If you're within reasonable driving distance, do a dry run with your vehicle or take public transportation to the interview location. Sometimes interview locations are different than the office locations, so always double check.

Note how long it took you to get there, check out the parking options (don't forget money if it's metered), and consider the traffic situation. Map an alternate route in case of bad traffic, have a cab company on speed dial or the Uber app available, and leave early enough to get there fifteen minutes early. This gives you time to check in, check your hair and clothes ensuring everything's where it should be, silence your phone, and take in the company atmosphere before show time.

Ultimately, the more you plan for your interviews, the more confidence and less anxiety you're going to have. As an applicant, this means you're more likely to deliver enticing information to your interviewers while relaxing enough to have a few friendly smiles or share a nerdy coding joke amidst the hours of hardcore and serious tech talk. Building rapport like this is so important—early impressions matter! If you find your mind wandering or casting self-doubt, remind yourself that the company simply wants to confirm that you're the right choice for the job.

Chapter 9

The Follow-up

You survived the seemingly endless rounds of interviews and are so exhausted from explaining block scoping you could scream – but you don't, because you're tired. These draining activities are all done, and now comes the "hurry up and wait" segment of the employment process.

You're bouncing off the wall with anticipation, yet companies rarely give you a deadline for when they'll get back to you. The world is fast, your mind is racing faster, and it's time to jump-start this discovery process.

Writing a Follow-up Message

Follow-up messages let you do a few things. First, they tell the company you're still interested in the job. Second, they emphasize your communication skills. Third, they give you an opportunity to include any information about yourself you might have left out of the interview, and/or clarify something you said. Fourth, they let you invite the interviewers to get in touch with you if they have further questions. All of these elements form a follow-up email that places yourself ahead of other candidates.

Here's a sample follow-up email:

Fullstack Web Dev Interview   _ ↗ ×

RosaRosarondaRosemary@rosss.com

Fullstack Web Dev Interview

Hi Rosa,

Thanks for meeting with me on Tuesday. It was great getting to meet you and learning more about the company.

I'm very much still interested in the fullstack web developer position. Plus, I just started playing around with Sequelize and am absolutely loving it for PostgreSQL. No wonder you listed this as a nice-to-have skill! :)

If you have any more questions about anything, I would be happy to answer them.

Thanks again, and looking forward to talking soon.

Jonas

Follow-up emails reinforce your interest in the job while highlighting your assertiveness.

Chapter 10

Job Offer & Salary Negotiation

A week goes by since your follow-up, and you can't help but obsessively check your email. Then *two* weeks. Then three weeks...Still nothing from the company.

Any minute that goes by where you don't hear from them is a minute too long. But finally, just when you were on the verge of losing hope, you check your email for the countless time this week and your stomach flutters with excitement.

It's a message from Human Resources.

Just like with the application process, there are two potential messages contained inside:

Scenario One: "We really enjoyed getting to know you, but we had to make the difficult decision to go forward with another candidate at this time..."

It's a rejection letter. Your stomach sinks even further. You tried your best and still didn't make it – is there a worse feeling? Give yourself some time to process the rejection, and when you're back on your feet, start investigating. Don't consider this experience a failure! Email members of the interview team and ask them if there is anything in particular you could work on to improve your chances as a candidate.

You might feel emotional when you're contacting team members, but *always keep follow-ups professional*. The quickest way to burn bridges and not get the feedback you want is to use language that is passive-aggressive, dramatic, or defensive. Stay positive and use their feedback to improve yourself.

Scenario Two: you got the job.

YOU.

GOT.

THE.

JOB.

Your hard work has paid off and your head is filled with a whirling cloud of thoughts. *When do I start? Who's my boss going to be? What am I getting paid?*

But wait...what *are* you getting paid? A dollar amount wasn't specified in the job listing and you never talked about it with your interview team. There is no salary listed in the congratulatory message, either. Uh oh. This smells like salary negotiation.

Salary negotiation can mean the difference between low-wage earnings and a well-appointed salary that is aligned with (or even above) the industry standard. While negotiation skills are helpful, you don't have to be a business expert to strike a deal.

Salary Negotiation is Awkward

As self-professed nerds, it's usually our job to make the internet work efficiently and beautifully, not haggle over dollar amounts. But tech companies exist to make money while saving money, and that includes saving money on your tech salary.

There are many books and other resources that share the art of the deal. However, those materials are more geared towards real estate barons, Wall Street investors, and other disciplines where multimillion-dollar deals are not uncommon. For web developers, however, it's time to get simple yet strategic.

Here's one method. Remember all those jobs you applied to on Deployment Day in Chapter Six? Certainly a few of them got back to you for an interview. And there's a chance that a few of those even landed in a job offer.

How much did they offer you?

What was the highest amount?

If you didn't talk with them yet about salary, what amount was listed on the job listing (or listed on Paysa or Glassdoor)?

Use these other job offers as leverage.

In other words, as the job offers come in, you collect the numbers and use them to your advantage.

This is why it's so important to never commit to your job offer right away. If you're not an aggressive negotiator (most of us aren't), simply say, "Thank you for the offer. I have a few other offers on the table right now, and need to think about it for a day or two. Your company stands out to me and I really want this to work. I think I can add a lot of value (I enjoyed meeting with you all, you have great coffee, etc.). Can I call back on (insert day in very near future) and speak with you?"

At this point, there's a good chance that of all the employers that offered you a job, you have your top pick in mind. Maybe they offer really good benefits and have a work culture you can relate to. Focus on assessing the salaries of your other offers along with their benefits packages and other employee perks.

Now, let's say your top pick employer is on the phone with you after a job offer sent via email. She congratulates you, there's the friendly small talk, and then it's down to business. "We offer a competitive salary starting at $45,000 along with partial medical and dental. We also offer unlimited stressballs, a reduced-price phone plan for you and your significant other…"

Your heart sinks. The company is located in a city with a higher cost of living and this wasn't the number the internet articles promised!

Asserting Your Worth

For introverts, this is where you must momentarily emerge from introversion to tell your new employer what you're worth. The whole process can be uncomfortable, and if you dislike confrontation, it's going to be even more unpleasant. However, if you start doubting yourself, think about your coding journey and just how hard you've studied and practiced to get to this point. Did you really practice web development every night for a year after work and build creative projects that efficiently and beautifully solved problems to get paid $45,000 (before taxes!) and no major benefits? Of course not. You made it this far; don't sell yourself short.

Here's the strategy you might use to navigate your way to a bigger, better paycheck. It's simple, and it works.

Recall the other salaries companies offered you, and reference the highest one. If the highest offer is below your area's average, or if you don't have any competing offers with dollar amounts, use the area's average. This may require research beyond Google (ask people at Meetups, your tech mentor, Reddit, etc. what a good salary is for the area if you can't find it).

On the phone with that company, when it comes down to the moment of truth, say, "If you can do $57,000, I'll accept the offer right away." Proceed to remind the employer what skills you can bring to the company to help make money and save money. A $12,000 difference in a $45,000 salary is nearly a 27% increase – not bad. That said, your company can certainly afford it.

Now It's the Company's Move

It's the company's turn. The company may choose to accept your proposal, suggest a counteroffer, or stick with their original offer.

If they accept your proposal: fantastic! Congrats, you've got yourself a new job!

If they counteroffer: weigh your options. If their counteroffer is still below an acceptable amount to you, ask if they'll be willing to throw in an extra perk like a day of remote work, or something else outside the scope of their regular benefits package. Or, if you feel like flexing your negotiation chops, counteroffer their counteroffer.

Finally, if they stick with their original offer: stay positive. Getting lowballed is disappointing, but it doesn't mean you're out of options. Sure, your top company pick is sticking firmly to a lower-than-average salary than normal, but is this a place where you see yourself growing and taking on valuable web developer tasks? Developing leadership skills? Expanding your skillset? It still may be worth it.

You can always ask for a raise a few months into the job if you're exceeding expectations. Further, if your salary is still in the slums, nothing is stopping you from commanding more money from another company after a year (or whatever your commitment) at this one. Take some time to reflect on your life, your goals, and your monetary needs.

Again, salary negotiation is awkward, but this process is **expected** in the labor market. If you're worried about upsetting somebody by asking for an increase in starting salary (even if it's a small business), stop. By *not* negotiating, you're cheapening your dream and selling yourself short.

Finally, *get your final salary amount in writing*. Not doing so can potentially set you up for failure when you get your first paycheck and the math doesn't add up, leading to problems of infinite varieties.

Chapter 11

Your First Week on the Job

You got the job and you're scheduled to start next Monday. It's Wednesday night, and you can't stop thinking about what to expect on your first day – and even week – at work as a web developer. Nervousness is natural, but to help ease you in with a little more confidence, here are some things you'll most likely be doing that first week:

1. Orientation. The time-honored tradition of meeting your bosses, co-workers, and random employees one floor below you that you may never see again. Employee badge, office tour, paperwork. No tech skills are required for this one, except perhaps an iron will to get through the training videos.

2. Setting up your development environment. This one takes a while, and things will go wrong. Be patient, have a positive attitude, and bear through one more hard restart when your machine is giving you hell. This week is largely reserved for untangling the major kinks of your workflow inherent in all new employee on-boarding.

3. You may have a chance to investigate the codebase(s). You'll be maintaining and updating this code, so take note of things like file structure, naming conventions, and any coding standards the developers follow.

Some other skills and items during your first week:

- **SSH key generation** (used for remoting into your company's and clients' machines)
- **Basic to intermediate command line operations** for creating folders, switching directories, copying projects to your local machine, granting permissions, etc.
- **Slack** (or other form of group messaging) – get familiar with Markdown syntax
- **Basic to intermediate Git** or whatever version control your company uses

Everything will be new for you; take notes and ask a *lot* of questions. This first week will be one of the few where you're not expected to Google the answers when you get stuck – never be shy to ask your trainers to clarify information.

76

You Made it to the End

You made it through the first week on the job. You're in! Your first paycheck will be another milestone, a reminder of your dedication and persistent focus. You look back and realize how many times you could have quit completely, how easy it could have been to stick to your old ways, but something inside you pushed you further. It's a great feeling and well-deserved.

Chapter 12

Conclusion

This book has given you a roadmap for starting a rewarding career in web development. From polishing your holy clover materials to developing your communication skills; asking and answering questions at interviews to crafting quality follow-ups; all the way to negotiating your salary and surviving your first week on the job, you are ready to confidently claim your spot in the tech industry as a junior web developer.

Your first job in a new career field is one of the hardest ones to get, so congratulations on a job well done. Your patience, persistence, and good old-fashioned hard work has finally paid off!

You've fought and pushed your way to the finish line. The *first* finish line, anyway. The world of tech is a never-ending journey with countless stops and detours, so take some time to enjoy the ride.

Appendix A: Where to Find Coding Questions and Challenges

- With over 35,000 GitHub stars at the time of this book's publication, h5pb's list of frontend developer interview questions are red-hot with popularity – and for good reason. This repo contains banks of questions ranging from JavaScript, to networking, to HTML and CSS, to testing and performance, and much more. Not to be missed! https://github.com/h5bp/Front-end-Developer-Interview-Questions

- Want to participate in mock interviews while being thrown real-life coding interview questions? https://www.pramp.com is your place. Pramp lets you hone those interview skills while experiencing the pressure of a simulated interview environment.

- Algorithms are tricky little beasts. https://www.codewars.com lets you practice them in an interactive environment. You code in your browser, syntax highlighting included, and use test cases as you progress.

- Focusing on JavaScript questions that require a narrative answer, https://www.tutorialspoint.com/javascript/javascript_interview_questions.htm spans from the fundamental "What is JavaScript?" to how to delete cookies.

- For PHP developers, https://www.codementor.io/blog/php-interview-questions-sample-answers-du1080ext gives you 25 questions that require code and narrative answers. Sample question: What are the main error types in PHP and how do they differ?

Appendix B: Where to Find Legitimate Web Developer Job Listings Online

- https://stackoverflow.com/jobs
- https://www.indeed.com
- https://www.linkedin.com/jobs/
- https://css-tricks.com/jobs/
- https://vuejobs.com
- https://jobs.github.com/positions
- Individual tech companies' websites

Appendix C: Minimizing Discrimination

People judge.

You could be the most successful and powerful person in the world, parting the seas and setting the sun with a simple verbal command, but there would still be *that* person who has a problem with your profile picture on LinkedIn. *Your hair is too natural. You're too light. Too dark. Not dark enough. Not skinny enough. Too old. Too young. Too gay. Are you gay? Too religious. Not enough tattoos. Good tattoos, who did your artwork, but was the hula girl **that** necessary?*

We want to minimize the chances of employers acting on their rudest instincts, but it's not like we can avoid showing our personal and genetic traits. They kind of come out at the job interview! Yet, discrimination is a reality during the pre-interview applicant selection process. What can a person do?

Perhaps the most prevalent kind of discrimination in tech is age-related. This doesn't mean you should stop applying to developer jobs or go to extremes like having your significant other help you with an emergency hair dye job. You're not hiding who you are, but what you *are* doing is reducing your chances of discrimination. Here's how to do it:

- Remove graduation dates and any other date that may portray your age.
- Update your legacy email address. Yahoo, AOL, Hotmail, etc. are red flags that you're not up-to-date.
- Don't go back more than 15 years on your job history. Not even soft skills age well and any web-related skill you practiced is now most definitely out of date.
- Make non-tech-related social media accounts private. Note that employers can still see your profile picture on most private accounts.

Other forms of bias are just as rude and dejecting. While it's impossible to go over every form of it, here are some additional ideas for avoiding discrimination in the application process:

- Some tech companies request a personal photo to be attached to your application materials. Don't accommodate the request; it's purely a discrimination tool.

- You don't necessarily need to list your state or city when applying to jobs, at least with the holy clover materials you submit.
- If you've volunteered to organize a political campaign and listed that on your resume (for example, to highlight your leadership skills), don't include the political party. You can use vague language and still have the same effect, such as "local non-profit organization" instead of "the XYZ Political Party."
- Keep your personal life out of your application materials.

Made in the USA
Las Vegas, NV
20 August 2021